Monica and Augustine

Blessed Are They Who Mourn

Monica: 332–387	Augustine: 354–430
Born in Tagaste, North Africa	Born in Tagaste, North Africa
Feast Day: August 27	Feast Day: August 28
Patron of Wives and Mothers	Patron of Theologians

"Blessed are they who mourn, for they shall be comforted."
Matthew 5:4

Text by Barbara Yoffie
Illustrated by Chris Sharp

Dedication

To my family:
my parents Jim and Peg,
my husband Bill,
our son Sam and daughter-in-law Erin,
and our precious grandchildren
Ben, Lucas, and Andrew

To all the children I have had the privilege of teaching throughout the years.

Imprimi Potest:
Kevin Zubel, CSsR, Provincial
Denver Province, the Redemptorists

Published by Liguori Publications, Liguori, Missouri 63057
To order, visit Liguori.org or call 800-325-9521.

ISBN (print): 978-0-7648-2867-6
ISBN (digital): 978-0-7648-7250-1

Liguori Publications, a nonprofit corporation, is a ministry of the Redemptorists. To learn more about the Redemptorists, visit Redemptorists.com.

Printed in the United States of America
28 27 26 25 24 / 5 4 3 2 1
First Edition

Dear Parents and Teachers:

Saints and Me! is a six-set series of children's books about saints, including: *Saints of North America* who served our homeland; *Saints of Christmas*, who teach us to love Jesus; *Saints for Families*, who modeled God's love within and for the domestic Church; *Saints for Communities*, who served Jesus through various roles and professions; and *Saints for Sacraments*, who showed great love for the sacraments.

The eight books in *Saints of the Beatitudes* (a word meaning "a list of blessings from God") introduce nine holy people who exemplify attributes Jesus articulated in his Sermon on the Mount. Faustina Kowalska's diary *Divine Mercy in My Soul,* read by millions, helped spread God's message of mercy. Patrick, a missionary, brought Christianity to Ireland. Monica prayed her wayward son, Augustine, would return to the faith. He did and was canonized. Katharine Drexel abandoned her comfortable life to become a nun. Carlo Acutis shared his faith and love of the Eucharist through technology. Bernadette Soubirous experienced visions of the Blessed Virgin Mary. Pope John XXIII convoked the Second Vatican Council, hoping to revive the Church. Jude was an apostle of our Lord.

Which saint was captured by pirates and sold into slavery? Name the saints with back-to-back feast days (August 27–28). Who gave $20 million to build churches and schools? Who created a website about eucharistic miracles? Who did Jesus appear and speak to? Who said, "My job is to inform, not to convince"? Who wrote *Peace on Earth* in 1963? Who is the patron of impossible causes? Find out in the *Saints of the Beatitudes* set—part of the *Saints and Me!* series—and help children connect to the lives of the saints.

Introduce your children or students to *Saints and Me!* as they:

—**READ** about the lives of the saints and are inspired by their stories.

—**PRAY** to the saints for their intercession.

—**CELEBRATE** the saints and relate them to their lives.

Free activities for children to use with this book may be downloaded at Liguori.org.

The Beatitudes

Divine blessings Jesus names in his Sermon on the Mount

Matthew 5:3–12

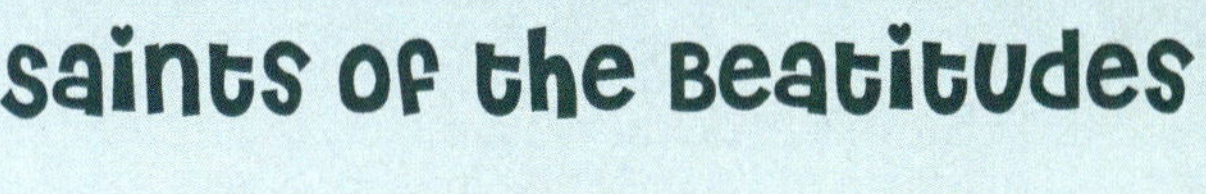

Saints of the Beatitudes

Patrick
Blessed Are the Poor in Spirit (Verse 3)

Monica and Augustine
Blessed Are They Who Mourn (Verse 4)

Katharine Drexel
Blessed Are the Meek (Verse 5)

Carlo Acutis
Blessed Are the Righteous (Verse 6)

Faustina Kowalska
Blessed Are the Merciful (Verse 7)

Bernadette
Blessed Are the Pure of Heart (Verse 8)

Pope John XXIII
Blessed Are the Peacemakers (Verse 9)

Jude the Apostle
Blessed Are the Persecuted (Verses 10–12)

Monica is the mother of Augustine, a great saint in the Catholic Church. Monica is a saint, too. She was a woman of great faith. She trusted God and prayed for her son, Augustine, when he did not want to follow the Christian faith. Monica was very sad that her son did not love God. After several years, her prayers were answered.

Born in northern Africa, Monica grew up in a Christian family, where she learned about prayer and the sacraments from her parents. She married a man named Patricius. He was not a Christian and did not believe in God. Monica loved God very much. *"Maybe someday I can teach my husband about the Christian faith,"* she thought.

Monica was a good wife and loved her husband. But her life with Patricius was not a happy one. He made fun of Monica when she prayed or helped someone in need. "Monica," he laughed, "why do you pray so much? It is a waste of time." "I like to pray. I feel at peace when I pray," she answered.

The mother of Patricius came to live with them. Monica hoped they would become good friends, but sadly his mother did not like her. Monica was patient and kind. She forgave them when they hurt her feelings.

She prayed for Patricius and his mother. It took a long time, but they saw the goodness in Monica and their hearts were changed. They wanted to be close to God, too, so they were baptized and became Christians.

Patricius and Monica had three children whom they loved very much. Monica wanted to keep her family close to God, but it was not easy. Their oldest son, Augustine, liked to play around and have fun.

Augustine made up stories and was lazy. He and his friends were always getting into trouble. "Oh, I wish you would listen to me! I worry about you all the time," Monica said with a sigh.

When Augustine was older, he
left home to go to school in the
city of Carthage. He and his new
friends made some bad choices.

Market

Monica was upset when she realized how much Augustine had changed. He did not follow the Christian faith. “God, please help my son give up his sinful ways.” She cried and prayed for Augustine every day.

After he finished school, Augustine went to Rome, Italy, to teach. Monica wanted to be close to him, so she decided to go to Rome, too.

Augustine did not like her idea. When she got to Rome, he was not there! Augustine had moved to Milan, Italy, for another teaching job. Monica did not give up! She went to Milan to find him.

Milan was a busy city. Augustine was excited to be teaching there. He met Bishop Ambrose, a great preacher who gave inspiring sermons. Augustine was interested in his ideas and learned many new things from Bishop Ambrose. Slowly, Augustine's heart and mind changed. "I was searching for God. Bishop Ambrose helped me find him."

Bishop Ambrose helped him to think about God in a different way. Day by day, he grew in his faith. Augustine realized that God was speaking to him when he read the Bible. “God was always in my heart and I know he loves me very much,” he admitted.

Monica found her son in the city of Milan and was with him when he was baptized on Easter. She was so happy! “Thank you, God, for answering my prayers,” she said. Monica never gave up hope that God would help Augustine become a man of great faith.

Augustine and his mother decided to return home to Africa. They spent a lot of time together talking about their faith, their love of God, and what heaven might be like. Monica found great joy in knowing that her son had given up his bad habits and had turned to God. She told Augustine, "My heart is at peace now. I know God has great plans for you." He smiled and gave her a big hug.

While waiting for a ship in the town of Ostia, Monica got very sick. Sadly, she died a few days later. Augustine was heartbroken. He loved his mother very much. He told his friends, "She was always ready to help me, even when I did not listen. My mother's prayers and tears led me back to God."

After returning to Africa, Augustine lived a prayerful and quiet life. He sold everything he owned and gave the money to the poor.

After a few years, he was ordained a priest. And later, he became the Bishop of Hippo, a town on the coast of Africa.

As bishop, he did many good things. He said Mass, preached, and cared for the poor and the sick. A brilliant teacher of the gospel, Bishop Augustine gave powerful sermons. He wrote many letters and books that told about his life and the great love he had for God.

His writings had a great influence on the Church and are important, even today. Augustine became one of the Church's greatest theologians, teaching and defending the Christian faith. The Church celebrates his feast day on August 28.

On August 27, the day before Augustine's feast day, we celebrate Monica. What a special way to honor saints who are mother and son! Monica shows us the power of prayer and how to trust God. Her love, patience, and kindness helped her family grow in holiness.

Our hearts are made for God above,
In him we find great peace and love.

♥ ♥ ♥

Saint Monica,

Your faith brought you comfort and peace.
When you were sad,
you prayed to God for help.
Help me to be patient
and wait for God's answer.

Saint Augustine,

You were open to God's calling.
You changed your bad habits
and turned back to God.
You faithfully taught
the message of the gospel.
Inspire me to share the gospel message
with others.

GLOSSARY (NEW WORDS)

Christian: One who follows Christianity, the religion founded on the life and teachings of Jesus Christ

Heartbroken: A feeling of great sadness

Mourn: To feel sad or sorrowful about someone or something

Ordained: To receive the sacrament of holy orders

Patient: To wait for something without getting upset or anxious

Sermon: A talk about religious teachings; also called a homily

Theologian: Someone who studies religious teachings and beliefs

Saints and me!

SAINTS FOR SACRAMENTS

Booklets in this set honored by the Association of Catholic Publishers!

John the Baptist:
Saint for Baptism
827969

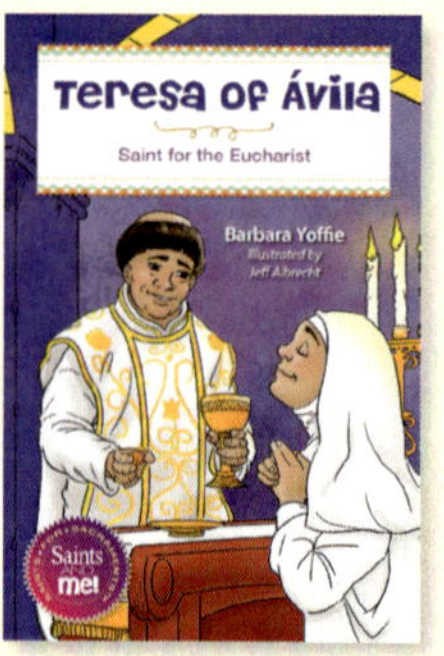

Teresa of Ávila:
Saint for the Eucharist
827938

Padre Pio:
Saint for Reconciliation
827921

Philip Neri:
Saint for Confirmation
827976

Maximilian Kolbe:
Saint for Anointing
of the Sick 827983

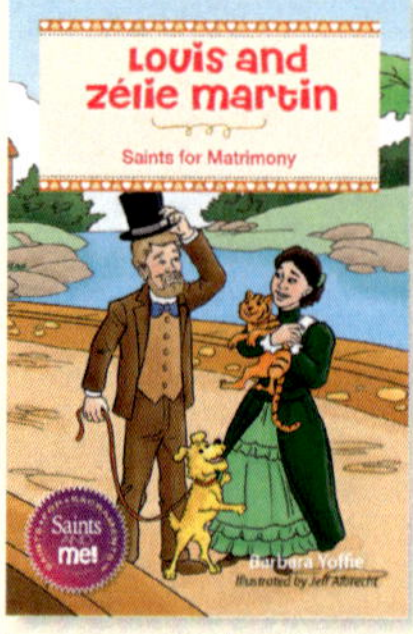

Louis and Zélie Martin:
Saints for Matrimony
827945

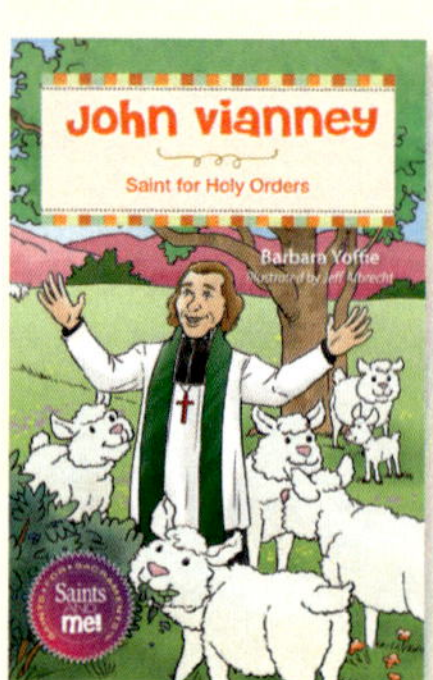

John Vianney:
Saint for Holy Orders
827952

Saints for Sacraments
Activity Book 828010

Get the Complete Set!

Saints for Sacraments
Collection A00085
(*Activity Book* sold separately)

Booklets: 32 pages, 5.5 x 8.5,
Full-color illustrations

Activity Book: 96 pages, 8.5 x 11

Order today! Call 800-325-9521 or visit Liguori.org.